Cooking Pancakes

by Anne Giulieri
photography by Ned Meldrum

You can cook pancakes.

Here is the flour.

Here is the milk.

Here is an egg.

Here is a bowl.

Here is a spoon.

Here is a pan.

The flour goes into the bowl.

PLAIN FLOUR

PLAIN FLOUR

The egg goes into the flour.

The milk
goes into the flour, too!

Here is a spoon.

The spoon goes
round and *round*.

Here is a pan.

The pan is hot.

Mum cooks the pancake.

This pancake is hot!
Look at the bubbles.

This banana
is for my pancake.

We are eating the pancakes!
Yum!